SERMON OUTLINES for

Evangelistic Services

The Bryant Sermon Outline Series

SERMON OUTLINES
for

Evangelistic Services

compiled by
Al Bryant

kregel
PUBLICATIONS

Grand Rapids, MI 49501

Sermon Outlines for Evangelistic Services
compiled by Al Bryant

© 1992 by Kregel Publications

Published by Kregel Publications, a division of Kregel, Inc.,
P.O. Box 2607, Grand Rapids, MI 49501. Kregel Publications
provides trusted, biblical publications for Christian growth and
service. Your comments and suggestions are valued.

For more information about Kregel Publications, visit our web
site at: www.kregel.com

Cover design: Frank Gutbrod

Library of Congress Cataloging-in-Publication
Sermon outlines for evangelistic services / compiled by Al
Bryant.
       p.   cm.
1. Evangelistic sermons—Outlines, syllabi, etc.
I. Bryant, Al.
BV3797.A1S47   1992   91-21641
251'.02—dc20

ISBN 0-8254-2054-7

2 3 4 5 / 04 03

Printed in the United States of America

CONTENTS

PREFACE

According to one definition, *Evangelism* is the proclamation of the good news of salvation in Jesus Christ with a view to bringing about the reconciliation of the sinner with God the Father, through the regenerating power of the Holy Spirit.

According to the comprehensive statement issued by the International Congress on World Evangelization in Lausanne in 1974, "To evangelize is to spread the good news that Jesus Christ died for our sins and was raised from the dead according to the Scriptures, and that as the reigning Lord He now offers the forgiveness of sins and the liberating gift of the Spirit to all who repent and believe."

The sermon outlines selected for this book are chosen for their clear presentation of the "good news" about Jesus Christ. They are designed for the understanding of those who perhaps attend church occasionally and have a rather nebulous relationship with the church. They are also chosen because of their clear presentation of the truths of the Gospel and the ramifications of a sincere belief in Jesus Christ as Savior and Lord. W. W. Sweet has said, "Evangelism stands for a certain interpretation of Christianity emphasizing the objective atonement of Christ, the necessity of a new birth, or conversion, and salvation through faith." The outlines in this book carry out that purpose.

Because of the format of the book, the user may choose simply to tear out a page and place the outline in his Bible. Or another option would be simply to photocopy the pages involved and make any additional notes in the margins, using that format to present the message.

It is not the purpose of the compiler to replace study on the part of the individual speaker who uses these outlines. Rather, these outlines are designed to be "pump primers" and "sermon starters." The user is encouraged to add his own personal illustrations and expositions of the various points in the outline. May you use these sermon outlines to the glory of God and the effective presentation of the Gospel.

AL BRYANT

TEXTUAL INDEX

MORAL INABILITY

"And Joshua said unto the people, Ye cannot serve the Lord" (*Joshua 24:19*).

In answer to Joshua's challenge, the people had said, "We will serve the Lord, for He is our God." But Joshua knew them too well to trust them, and reminded them that they were undertaking what they could not perform. They did not believe him, but cried, "Nay, but we will serve the Lord"; but their later history proved the truth of Joshua's warning. God's Word knows us better than we know ourselves. God's Omniscience sees each part of our being as an anatomist sees the various portions of the body, and He therefore knows our moral and spiritual nature most thoroughly. A watchmaker is the best judge of a watch; and He Who made man has the best knowledge of his condition and capacity. Let us dwell upon His verdict as to human ability.

I. **The Certainty of the Truth That Unrenewed Men Cannot Serve God.**

It is not a physical but a moral inability, and this is not in their nature, but in their fallen nature; not of God, but of sin.

1. The nature of God renders perfect service impossible to depraved man (see context, v. 19).

2. The best they could render as unrenewed men would lack heart and intent, and therefore must be unacceptable (Isa. 1:15).

3. The law of God is perfect, who can hope to fulfill it? If a look may commit adultery, who shall in all points keep the law? (Matt. 5:28).

4. The carnal mind is inclined to self-will, self-seeking, lust, enmity, pride, and all other evils (Rom. 8:7).

II. **The Discouragement Which Arises from This Truth.**

It is alleged that this will drive men to despair, and our reply is that the kind of despair to which it drives men is most desirable and beneficial.

1. It discourages men from an impossible task.

They might as well hope to invent perpetual motion as to present a perfect obedience of their own, having already sinned. If a man should try to hold up a ladder with his own hand, and at the same time climb to the top of it, he would have less difficulty than in causing his evil nature to attain to holiness.

2. It discourages from a ruinous course.

Self-righteousness is a deadly thing; it is a proud refusal of mercy, and a rebellion against grace. Self-confidence of any sort is the enemy of the Savior.

3. It discourages reliance upon ceremonies or any other outward religiousness, by assuring men that these cannot suffice.

4. It discourages from every other way of self-salvation, and thus shuts men up to faith in the Lord Jesus. Nothing better can befall them (Gal. 2:22,23).

III. The Necessities of Which We Are Reminded by This Truth.

Unregenerate men, before you can serve God you need: A new nature, which only the Spirit of God can create in you.

Reconciliation. How shall an enemy serve his king?

Acceptance. Till you are accepted, your service cannot please God.

Continued aid. This you must have to keep you in the way when once you are in it (1 Sam. 2:9; Jude 24:25).

- No wasp will make honey; before it will do that it must be transformed into a bee. A sow will not sit up to wash its face like the cat before the fire; neither will a debauched person take delight in holiness. No devil could praise the Lord as angels do, and no unregenerate man can offer acceptable service as the saints do.　　—George Bush, in *Notes on Joshua*

- "Man cannot be saved by perfect obedience, for he cannot render it; he cannot be saved by imperfect obedience, for God will not accept it."　　　—British Evangelist

- "Run, run, and work, the law commands,
  But gives me neither feet nor hands;
  But sweeter sounds the gospel brings,
  It bids me fly, and gives me wings."

C.H. SPURGEON

CLINGING TO THE ALTAR

"Joab fled unto the tabernacle of the Lord, and caught hold on the horns of the altar. . . .

"And Benaiah came to the tabernacle of the Lord, and said unto him, Thus saith the king, come forth. And he said, Nay; but I will die here" (1 Kings 2:28, 30).

Joab knew little enough of religion, yet he flies to the altar when the sword pursues him.

Many are for running to the use of external religion when death threatens them. Then they go to greater lengths than Scripture prescribes; they not only go to the tabernacle of the Lord but they must also cling to the altar.

I. An Outward Resort to Ordinances Does Not Win Salvation.

If a man will rest in external rites he will die there.

Sacraments, in health or in sickness, are unavailing as means of salvation. They are intended only for those saved already, and will be injurious to others (1 Cor. 11:29).

Ministers. These are looked upon by some dying persons with foolish reverence. In the hour of death resort is made to their prayers at the bedside. Importance is attached to funeral sermons and ceremonials. What superstition!

Feelings. Dread, delight, dreaminess, despondency; these have, each in its turn, been relied upon as grounds of hope; but they are all futile.

What an awful thing to perish with your hand on the altar of God!

II. A Spiritual Resort to the True Altar Opens the Heart to Salvation.

We will use Joab's case as an illustration.

1. His act; he "caught hold on the horns of the altar."

We do this spiritually by flying from the sword of justice to the person of Jesus and by taking hold upon His great atoning work, thus through faith uniting ourselves to His provision for our souls.

2. The fierce demand of His adversary. "Thus saith the king, Come forth!"

This is the demand of unbelieving Pharisees who teach salvation by works.

Accusing conscience within the man.
Satan, quoting Holy Scripture falsely.

3. The desperate resolve of Joab. "Nay, but I will die here." This is a wise resolution, for we:

Must perish elsewhere.
Cannot make our case worse by clinging to Christ.
Have nowhere else to cling. No other righteousness or sacrifice.
Cannot be dragged away if we cling to Jesus.
Receive hope from the fact that none have perished here.

4. The assured security. "He that believeth on the Son hath everlasting life" (John 3:36). If you perished trusting in Jesus your ruin would:

Defeat God.
Dishonor Christ.
Dishearten sinners from coming to Jesus.
Discourage saints, making them doubt all the promises.
Distress the glorified, who have rejoiced over penitents, and would now see that they were mistaken.

• Come, then, at once to the Lord Jesus, and lay hold on eternal life.
You may come; He invites you.
You should come; He commands you.
You should come now; for now is the accepted time.

• When a man goes thirsty to the well, his thirst is not allayed merely by going there. On the contrary, it is increased by every step he goes. It is by what he draws out of the well that his thirst is satisfied. Just so it is not by the mere bodily exercise of waiting upon ordinances that you will ever come to peace, but by tasting of Jesus in the ordinances, whose flesh is meat indeed, and His blood drink indeed.   —M'Cheyne.

• A pilot loves to get the helm in his hand, a physician delights to be trusted with hard cases, an advocate is glad to get his brief; even so is Jesus happy to be used. Jesus longs to bless, and therefore, He says to every sinner, as He did to the woman at the well, "Give Me to drink." Oh, to think that you can refresh your Redeemer! Poor sinner, haste to do it.

C.H. SPURGEON

THE SINNER'S SURRENDER TO HIS PRESERVER

"I have sinned; what shall I do unto Thee, O Thou preserver of men?" (Job 7:20).

Job could defend himself before men, but he used another tone when bowing before the Lord; there he cried, "I have sinned." The words would suit any afflicted saint; for, indeed, they were uttered by such an one; but they may also be used by the penitent sinner, and we will on this occasion direct them to that use.

I. A Confession. "I have sinned."

In words this is no more than a hypocrite, nay, a Judas, a Saul, a Balaam, might say. Do not many call themselves "miserable sinners" who are indeed despicable mockers? Yet seeing Job's heart was right his confession was accepted.

　1. It was personal. *I have sinned*, whatever others may have done.

　2. It was to the Lord. He addresses the confession not to his fellow-man but to the Preserver of men.

　3. It was a confession wrought by the Spirit. See verse 18, where he ascribes his grief to the visitation of God.

　4. It was feeling. He was cut to the quick by it. Read the whole chapter. This one fact, "I have sinned," is enough to brand the soul with the mark of Cain, and burn it with the flames of hell.

　5. It was a believing confession. Mingled with much unbelief, Job still had faith in God's power to pardon. An unbelieving confession may increase sin.

II. An Inquiry. "What Shall I Do Unto Thee?"

In this question we see:

　1. His willingness to do anything, whatever the Lord might demand, thus proving his earnestness.

　2. His bewilderment; he could not tell what to offer, or where to turn; yet something must be done.

　3. His surrender at discretion. He makes no conditions, he only begs to know the Lord's terms.

III. A Title. "O Thou Preserver of Men!"

Observer of men, therefore aware of my case, my misery, my confession, my desire for pardon, my utter helplessness.

Preserver of men.

By His infinite patience, refraining from punishment.

By daily bounties of supply, keeping the ungrateful alive.

By the plan of salvation, delivering men from going down into the pit, snatching the brands from the burning.

- No sooner had Job confessed his sin but he is desirous to know a remedy. Reprobates can cry, "I have sinned"; but then they proceed not to say as here, "What shall I do?" They open their wound, but lay not on a plaster, and so the wounds made by sin are more putrefied, and grow more dangerous. Job would be directed what to do for remedy; he would have pardoning grace and prevailing grace upon any terms.   —Trapp.

Job was one of those whom Scripture describes as "perfect," yet he cried, "I have sinned." Noah was perfect in his generation, but no drunkard will allow us to forget that he had his fault. Abraham received the command, "Walk before me and be thou perfect," but he was not absolutely sinless. Zacharias and Elizabeth were blameless, and yet there was enough unbelief in Zacharias to make him dumb for nine months.

The doctrine of sinless perfection in the flesh is not of God, and he who makes his boast of possessing such perfection has at once declared his own ignorance of himself and of the law of the Lord. Nothing discovers an evil heart more surely than a glorying in its own goodness. He who proclaims his own praise reveals his own shame.

Man is in himself so feeble a creature, that it is a great wonder that he has not long ago been crushed by the elements, exterminated by wild beasts, or destroyed by disease. Omnipotence has bowed itself to his preservation, and compelled all visible things to form the Body-guard of Man. We believe that the same Preserver of men Who has thus guarded the race watches with equal care over every individual.

The unconditional surrender implied in the question, "What shall I do unto Thee?" is absolutely essential from every man who hopes to be saved. God will never raise the siege until we hand out the keys of the city, open every gate, and bid the Conqueror ride through every street, and take possession of the citadel. The traitor must deliver up himself and trust the prince's clemency. Till this is done the battle will continue; for the first requisite for peace with God is complete submission.   C.H. SPURGEON

THE PENITENTIAL SACRIFICE

"The sacrifices of God are a broken spirit; a broken and a contrite heart, oh God, thou wilt not despise" (Psalm 51:17).

David, deeply humbled by his sin, compares his present state of mind to a sacrificial victim, ready to be offered upon the altar. Such victims were separated from the flock or herd, and set apart for God. The penitent also separates himself from customary fellowship and mourns apart. He no longer considers himself as his own, but the Lord's; to whom he now dedicates himself, by a solemn and voluntary devotion. Psalm 4:3. Romans 12:1. And as the typical sacrifices were put to death, in order to their being offered; so the penitent becomes dead to the world, and dead to sin, and is crucified together with Christ. The legal sacrifices were reiterated, year by year, and day by day, Hebrews 10:11. So, though there may be special occasions for repentance as in the case of David; yet the sacrifice of a broken heart, and of a contrite spirit, must be the daily offering of every sinner who seeks acceptance with God.

I. **Inquire What Is Included in This Spiritual Sacrifice.**

A broken and a contrite spirit is not merely one that is distressed, nor one that is distressed for sin. Rachel was distressed for her children, and Micah about his gods; but it had nothing to do with true repentance. Cain and Judas sank into despair, from a sense of guilt and wretchedness; but in them it was that kind of sorrow which results in death, and not repentance which is unto life (2 Cor. 7:10).

1. A truly contrite spirit is deeply affected with *the evil of sin*, as it dishonors God, and is injurious to ourselves and others. This is exemplified in the case of the Prodigal, Luke 15:21: in the case of the Publican, Luke 18:13: and in that of David in the context, v. 4. The conviction of such a penitent is, that he has ruined himself, beyond the power of the whole creation to redeem; that if God should utterly destroy him, the sentence would be just; and if saved it must be of unbounded grace and love, Ephesians 2:4,5. A broken spirit is deeply contrite, and almost in danger of being swallowed up of grief Psalm 38:3,4; 2 Corinthians 2:7.

2. A contrite spirit groans under the burden of *inherent corruption*, as well as of sins actually committed: vv. 5,6. A true penitent is made to know the plague of his own heart, and to cry out for deliverance. Romans 9:23,24. Hence some Christians, after they have

attained to a good hope through grace, and walked humbly with God for many years, complain more bitterly than ever of indwelling sin, and can find no relief but in the atoning blood. Those who seek justification from their own sanctification invert the order of the gospel; and it is impossible that imperfect obedience should yield perfect peace.

3. A broken and contrite spirit trembles at the least indications of *divine displeasure*—not only judgments inflicted, but judgments threatened or only apprehended, fill it with dismay. Isaiah 65:2; Psalm 119:120. A true penitent trembles more at God's Word than others do at His rod. 2 Chronicles 34:18, 27; Job 31:33.

4. A broken spirit patiently submits to the severest *chastisements*, and will bear the indignation of the Lord, from a conviction of having deserved it, and from the hope of future deliverance. Micah 7:9. When God smites, the penitent also smites, and is at all times disposed to take part with God against himself. He turns his cheek to him who strikes him, and lays his spirit in the dust. Lamentations 3:29,30; Jeremiah 31:18,19.

II. God's Gracious Acceptance of Such a Sacrifice.

This is expressed negatively; "a broken and a contrite spirit, oh God, Thou wilt not despise." It is so worthless in itself, consisting of nothing but the groans and tears of a brokenhearted penitent, that He might well despise it; but He will not. It is presented with so many imperfections, and in a manner so unworthy of His notice, that He might reject both offerer and sacrifice; but He will not—

1. Because He delights more in *showing mercy*, than in whole burnt offerings or sacrifices. If He accepted the sacrifices under the law, it was only as they pointed to the great atonement to be made in the end of the world, and as they were accompanied with the penitential confessions of the offerer. And now especially, as these sacrifices have ceased, He will accept that which is spiritual (1 Peter 2:5).

2. The sacrifices of a broken heart, offered up *in the name of Jesus*, cannot fail to be accepted, because they are perfumed with His incense, and presented through His intercession (Eph. 1:6; Rev. 8:4).

3. God has made *many promises* to the humble and the contrite, and has testified His acceptance of them and of their offering (Ps. 31:20, 147:3; Isa. 57:13). Consider Ephraim, (Jer. 31:20); the Publican, (Lk. 18:14); and the woman who was a sinner, Lk. 7:50. Be comforted: God will not despise the day of small things, nor let us despise it (Matthew 12:20).   Charles Simeon

THINGS ARE NOT WHAT THEY SEEM

"All the ways of a man are clean in his own eyes; but the Lord weigheth the spirits" (Proverbs 16:2).

Occasionally in seasons of depression and disaster great discoveries are made concerning those who appeared to be commercially sound but turn out to be rotten. All looked solid and substantial until the inevitable crash came, and then no man felt that he could trust his neighbor. No doubt these schemers thought their ways "clean," but the event exposed their dirty hands.

Spiritual failures of like kind occur in the church. Great reputations explode, high professions dissolve. Men readily cajole themselves into the belief that they are right, and are doing right. A weighing time comes and their professions are exposed.

I. **The Ways of the Openly Wicked. Many of these are "clean" in their own eyes.**
   To effect this self-deception:
   They give pretty names to sin.
   They think ill of others, making them out to be much worse than themselves, and finding in this an excuse for themselves.

II. **The Ways of the Outward Religionist. These seem "clean."**
   His observance of ceremonies.
   His regular attendance at worship.
   His open profession of religion.
   His generosity to the cause, and general interest in good things.
   Thus ministers, deacons, members, etc., may boast, and yet, when the Lord weighs their spirits, they may be castaways.

III. **The Ways of the Worldly Professor. He thinks himself "clean."**
   Let him honestly consider whether he is "clean":
   In his secret life? In his private and hidden indulgences?
   In his pleasures and amusements?
   In his company and conversation?
   In his forsaken closet, forgotten Bible, lukewarm religion, etc.
   What a revelation when the weighing of his spirit comes!

IV. **The Ways of the Secure Backslider. He dreams that his way is "clean," when a little observation will show him many miry places:**

Decline in private prayer (Job 15:4).
Sin gradually getting the upper hand (Jer. 15:10).
Conversation scantily spiritual (Eph. 5:4).
Scriptures little read (Hos. 8:12).
Heart growing hard (Heb. 3:13).

How beautiful all things look when winter has bleached them! What royal bed is to be seen in yonder corner! The coverlet is whiter than any fuller on earth could white it! Here might an angel take his rest, and rise as pure as when he reclined upon it. In reality, it is a dunghill, and nothing more.

All the ships that came into the harbor were claimed by one person in the city. He walked the quay with a right royal air, talked largely about owning a navy, and swaggered quite sufficiently had it been so. How came he to be so wealthy? Listen, he is a madman. He has persuaded himself into this folly, but in truth he has not a tub to call his own. What absurdity! Are not many the victims of even worse self-deception? They are rich and increased in goods according to their own notion; yet they are naked, and poor, and miserable.

"This must be the right way, see how smooth it is! How many feet have trodden it!" Alas! that is precisely the mark of the broad road which leads to destruction.

"But see how it winds about, and what a variety of directions it takes! It is no bigot's unbending line." Just so; therein it proves itself to be the wrong road; for truth is one and unchanging.

"But I like it so much." This also is suspicious; for what an unrenewed man is so fond of is probably an evil thing. Hearts go after that which is like themselves, and graceless men love graceless ways.

"Would you have me go that narrow and rough road?" Yes, we would; for it leads unto life; and though few there be that find it, yet those who do so declare that it is a way of pleasantness. It is better to follow a rough road to heaven than a smooth road to hell.

C.H. SPURGEON

INVITATION TO A CONFERENCE

"Come now, and let us reason together, saith the Lord: though your sins be as scarlet, they shall be as white as snow; though they be red like crimson, they shall be as wool" (Isaiah 1:18).

The sinful condition of men is terrible in the extreme. This is set forth vividly in previous verses of the chapter. They are altogether alienated from their God.

I. An Invitation to a Conference.

Sinful men do not care to think, consider, and look matters in the face; yet to this distasteful duty they are urged. If they reason, they rather reason against God than together with Him; but here the proposal is not to discuss, but to treat with a view of reconciliation. This also ungodly hearts decline.

1. They prefer to attend to ceremonial observances. Outward performances are easier, and do not require thought.

2. Yet the matter is one which demands most serious discussion, and deserves it; for God, the soul, heaven, and hell are involved in it. Never was wise counsel more desirable.

3. It is most gracious on the Lord's part to suggest a conference. Kings do not often invite criminals to reason with them.

4. The invitation is a pledge that He desires peace, is willing to forgive, and anxious to set us right.

II. A Specimen of the Reasoning on God's Part.

1. The one main ground of difference is honestly mentioned—"though your sins be as scarlet." God calls the most glaring sinners to come to Him, knowing them to be such.

2. This ground of difference God Himself will remove—"they shall be as white as snow." He will forgive, and so end the quarrel.

3. He will remove the offense perfectly—"as snow—as wool."
He will remove forever the guilt of sin.
He will discharge the penalty of sin.
He will destroy the dominion of sin.
He will prevent the return of sin.

III. This Specimen Reasoning Is an Abstract of the Whole Argument.

Each special objection is anticipated.

1. The singular greatness of your sins—"red like crimson." This is met by a great atonement, which cleanses from all sin.

2. The long continuance of your sins. Cloth dyed scarlet has lain long in the dye-vat. The blood of Jesus cleanses at once.

3. The light against which your sins were committed. This puts a glaring color upon them. But "all manner of sin and blasphemy shall be forgiven unto men."

4. The despair which your sins create: they are so glaring that they are ever before you, yet they shall be washed out by the blood of the Lamb of God, which taketh away the sin of the world.

Certain scarlet cloth is first dyed in the grain, and then dyed in the piece; it is thus double-dyed. And so are we with regard to the guilt of sin; we are double-dyed for we are all sinners by birth, and sinners by practice. Our sins are like scarlet, yet by faith in Christ they shall be as white as snow: by an interest in Christ's atonement, though our offenses be red like crimson, they shall be as wool; that is, they shall be as white as the undyed wool.

- Consider how the Tyrian scarlet was dyed; not superficially dipped, but thoroughly drenched in the liquor that colored it, as the soul in custom of sinning. Then was it taken out for a time and dried, put in again, soaked and sodden the second time in the vat; called therefore twice-dyed; as you complain you have been by relapsing into the same sin. Yea, the color so incorporated into the cloth, not drawn over, but diving into the very heart of the wool, that, rub a scarlet rag on what is white, and it will bestow a reddish tincture upon it; as perchance, your sinful practice and precedent have also infected those who were formerly good, by your badness. Yet such scarlet sins, so solemnly and substantially colored, are easily washed white in the blood of our Savior.   —Thomas Fuller
C.H. SPURGEON

"A man shall be as an hiding-place from the wind, and a covert from the tempest" (Isaiah 32:28).

Immense boons have come to nations by kings like David, prophets like Samuel, deliverers like Gideon, lawgivers like Moses.

But what are all good men put together compared with *The Man* Christ Jesus?

Let us consider that—

I. This Life Is Liable to Storms.

1. Mysterious hurricanes within, which cause the most dreadful confusion of mind.

2. Overwhelming tempests of spiritual distress on account of sin.

3. Wild attacks from human enemies, who taunt, slander, threaten, etc.

4. Trying gales of temporal losses, bereavements, and other afflictions.

II. From These Storms the Man Christ Jesus Is Our Hiding-Place.

1. As truly Man. Sympathizing with us.

2. As more than Man, ruling every tempest.

3. As Substitutionary Man.

In Him we are delivered from divine wrath.

In Him we are covered from Satan's blasts.

In Him we dwell above trial by happy fellowship with Him.

In Him we are victors over death.

4. As the Coming Man. We dread no political catastrophes, or social disruptions, for "He must reign." The end is secured. "Behold, He cometh with clouds" (Rev. 1:7).

III. Let Us See to It That We Take Shelter in the Man.

1. Let Him stand before us, interposing Himself between us and the punishment of sin. Hide behind Him by faith.

2. Let Him daily cover us from all evil, as our Shield and Protector (Ps. 119:114).

O you that are out of Christ, the tempest is lowering! Come to this covert; hasten to this hiding-place!

He is a capacious hiding-place: "Yet there is room." As in

Adullam all David's army could hide, so is Jesus able to receive hosts of sinners.

- I creep under my Lord's wings in the great downpour, and the waters cannot reach me. Let fools laugh the fools' laughter, and scorn Christ, and bid the weeping captives in Babylon to sing them one of the songs of Zion. We may sing, even in our winter's storm, in the expectation of a summer's sun at the turn of the year. No created powers in hell, or out of hell, can mar our Lord's work, or spoil our song of joy. Let us then be glad and rejoice in the salvation of our Lord, for faith had never yet cause to have tearful eyes, or a saddened brow, or to droop or die. —Samuel Rutherford

A shelter is nothing if we stand in front of it. The main thought with many a would-be Christian is his own works, feelings, and attainments: this is to stand on the windy side of the wall by putting self before Jesus. Our safety lies in getting behind Christ, and letting Him stand in the wind's eye. We must be altogether hidden, or Christ cannot be our hiding-place.

Foolish religionists hear about the hiding-place, but never get into it. How great is the folly of such conduct. It makes Jesus to be of no value or effect. What is a roof to a man who lies in the open, or a boat to one who sinks in the sea? Even the Man Christ Jesus, though ordained of God to be a covert from the tempest, can cover none but those who are in Him. Come then, poor sinner, enter where you may; hide in Him Who was evidently meant to hide you, for He was ordained to be a hiding-place, and must be used as such, or the very aim of His life and death would be missed.

C.H. SPURGEON

"Then You Ask Him"

Said Dr. Carl F. H. Henry, "In one of my last street meetings, during my college years, a heckler kept shouting, 'Where did Cain get his wife?'

"When I could ignore the disturber no longer. I replied, 'When I get to heaven, I'll ask him!'

"'Suppose he isn't in heaven?' parried the disrupter.

"I retorted. 'Then you can ask him!'"

REPENTANCE

"Let the wicked forsake his way, and the unrighteous man his thoughts: and let him return unto the Lord, and He will have mercy upon him" (Isaiah 55:7).

This is the great chapter of gospel invitation. How free! How full! How plain and pressing are the calls to receive grace!

I. The Necessity of Conversion.

1. *The nature of God.* How can a holy God wink at sin, and pardon sinners who continue in their wickedness?

2. *The nature of the gospel.* It is not a proclamation of tolerance for sin, but of deliverance from it. It contains no single promise of forgiveness to the man who goes on in his iniquity.

3. *The facts of the past.* No instance has occurred of pardon given to man while obstinately persisting in his evil way. Conversion always goes with salvation.

4. *The well-being of the sinner himself* requires that he should quit his sin, or feel its penalty. To be favored with a sense of divine pardon, while obstinately abiding in sin, would confirm the man in sin; and sin itself is a worse evil than its penalty.

II. The Nature of Conversion.

1. It deals with the life and conduct. The man's "way." His natural way; that into which he runs when left to himself.

   His habitual way; to which he is accustomed.

   His beloved way; wherein his pleasures lie.

   The general way; the broad road in which the many run.

   This, our text says, he must "forsake." He must have done with sin, or he will be undone. It will not suffice for him to—

   Own that it is wrong;

   Profess to be sorry for following it;

   Resolve to leave it, and end in resolve, or

   Move more cautiously in it.

   No, he must forsake it altogether, at once, and forever.

2. It deals with the "thoughts." A man must forsake—

   His unscriptural opinions, and self-formed notions—

   About God, His law, His gospel, His people.

   About sin, punishment, Christ, self, etc.

3. It deals with the man in reference to God. "Let him return unto the Lord."

It bids him cease from pride, neglect, opposition, distrust, disobedience, and all other forms of alienation from the Lord. He must turn and return: wandering no further, but coming home.

III. The Gospel of Conversion.
1. A sure promise is made to it. "He will have mercy upon him."
2. The pardon which comes with it is the result of a full atonement, which renders the pardon abundant, just, safe, and easy of belief to the awakened conscience.

Oh, that the sinner would consider the need of a total change of thought within, and way without! It must be thorough and radical or it will be useless.

Total and terrible ruin must ensue if you continue in evil.

May this house see the turning-point in your life's course! God says, "Let him return." What hinders you?

William Burns was preaching one evening in the open air, to a vast multitude. He had just finished, when a man came timidly up to him, and said, "O Sir! will you come and see my dying wife?" Burns consented; but the man immediately said, "Oh! I am afraid when you know where she is you won't come." "I will go wherever she is," he replied.

The man then tremblingly told him that he was the keeper of the lowest inn in one of the most wretched districts of the town. "It does not matter," said the missionary, "come away." As they went, the man, looking up in the face of God's servant, said earnestly, "O Sir! I am going to give it up at the term." Burns replied, "There are no terms with God." However much the poor trembling publican tried to get Burns to converse with him about the state of his soul, and the way of salvation, he was unable to draw another word from him than these—"There are no terms with God."

The shop was at last reached. They passed through it in order to reach the chamber of death. After a little conversation with the dying woman, the servant of the Lord engaged in prayer, and while he was praying the publican left the room, and soon a loud noise was heard, something like a rapid succession of determined knocks with a great hammer. Was this not a most unseemly noise to make on such a solemn occasion as this? Is the man mad? No.

When Burns reached the street, he beheld the wreck of the innkeeper's sign board strewn in splinters upon the pavement. The business was given up for good and all. The man had in earnest turned his back on his low form of livelihood, and returned to the Lord, who had mercy upon him, and unto our God, who abundantly pardoned all his sins. Nothing transpired in his after-life to discredit the reality of his conversion.   —William Brown, in *"Joyful Sound."*

C.H. SPURGEON

DECIDED UNGODLINESS

"They have refused to return" (Jeremiah 5:3).

I. Who Have Refused to Return?

1. Those who have said as much. With unusual honesty or presumption, they have made public declaration that they will never quit their sinful ways.

2. Those who have made a promise to repent, but have not performed it.

3. Those who have offered other things instead of practical return to God: ceremonies, religiousness, morality, and the like.

4. Those who have only returned in appearance. Formalists, mere professors, and hypocrites.

II. What This Refusal Unveils.

1. An intense love of sin.

2. A want of love to the great Father, Who bids them return.

3. A despising of God: they reject His counsel, His command, and even Himself.

4. A resolve to continue in evil. This is their proud ultimatum, "they have refused to return."

5. A trifling with serious concerns. They are too busy, too fond of fun, etc. There is time enough yet.

III. What Is the Real Reason of This Refusal?

1. It may be self-conceit: perhaps they dream that they are already on the right road.

2. It is at times sheer recklessness. The man refuses to consider his own best interest. He resolves to be a trifler; death and hell and heaven are to him as toys to sport with.

3. It is a dislike of holiness. That lies at the bottom of it: men cannot endure humility, self-denial, and obedience to God.

4. It is a preference for the present above the eternal future.

From the cross the Lord Jesus calls you on to return. Hasten home!

- The door of heaven shuts from below, not from above. "Your iniquities have separated," saith the Lord. —Williams, *of Wern*

- Lord Byron, a short time before death, was heard to say, "Shall I sue for mercy?" After a long pause, he added, "Come, come, no weakness; let's be a man to the last!"

- The reason why a wicked man does not turn unto God is not because he cannot (though he cannot), but because he will not. He cannot say at the day of judgment, "Lord, Thou knowest I did my best to be holy, but I could not." The man who didn't have a wedding garment could not say, "Lord, I was not able to get one." But he was "speechless."   —W. Fenner

C.H. SPURGEON

THE EVIL OF SIN

Jeremiah 2:19

I.   The Prophet's Description of Sin
Sin here is summed up in two things: "forsaking the Lord our God" and "His fear not being in us."
   A.   Every sinner has forsaken God.
   B.   As God is not loved, so neither is He feared.
   C.   From these two sources proceed all the evils that are in the world.

II.   The Evil and Bitter Nature of Sin
We may "know and see" by—
   A.   The precepts of God's holy law.
   B.   The awful threatenings of God's Word.
   C.   The bitter sorrows of true penitents.
   D.   The bitter fruits it produces.
   E.   The still more bitter fruits it would produce, if God did not restrain it.
   F.   The bitter pains of eternal death.
   G.   The bitter sufferings of the Son of God.

III.   The Exhortation
Unless we "know and see"—
   A.   We can neither know nor see the salvation of God.
   B.   We shall neither repent of sin nor depart from it.
   C.   We shall be made to know and see it to our cost in the world to come.   CHARLES SIMEON

MISTAKEN NOTIONS ABOUT REPENTANCE

"And I will multiply the fruit of the tree, and the increase of the field, that ye shall receive no more reproach of famine among the heathen. Then shall ye remember your own evil ways, and your doings that were not good, and shall loathe yourselves in your own sight for your iniquities, and for your abominations" (Ezekiel 36:30,31).

Repentance is wrought in the heart by a sense of love divine.

This sets repentance in its true light, and helps us to meet a great many mistakes which have darkened this subject. Many are kept from Christ and hope by misapprehensions of this matter. They have—

I. Mistaken Ideas of What Repentance Is.

They confound it with—

1. Morbid *self-accusation*, which is the fruit of dyspepsia, or melancholy, or insanity. This is an infirmity of mind, and not a grace of the Spirit. A physician may here do more than a divine.

2. *Unbelief, despondency, despair:* which are not even a help to repentance, but tend rather to harden the heart.

3. Dread of hell, and sense of wrath: which might occur even to devils, and yet would not cause them to repent. A measure of this may go with repentance, but it is no part of it.

Repentance is

- a hatred of evil
- a sense of shame
- a longing to avoid sin
- Wrought by a sense of divine love.

II. Mistaken Ideas of the Place Which Repentance Occupies.

1. It is looked upon by some as a procuring cause of grace, as if repentance merited remission: a grave error.

2. It is wrongly viewed by others as a preparation for grace; a human goodness laying the foundation for mercy, a meeting of God half way; this is a deadly error.

3. It is treated as a sort of qualification for believing, and even as the ground for believing: all which is legality, and contrary to pure gospel truth.

4. Others treat it as the argument for peace of mind. They

have repented so much, and it must be all right. This is to build our confidence upon a false foundation.

III. Mistaken Ideas of the Way in Which It Is Produced in the Heart.

It is not produced by a distinct and immediate attempt to repent. Nor by strong excitement at revival meetings.

Nor by meditating upon sin, and death, and hell, etc.

But the God of all grace produces it—

1. By His free grace, which by its action renews the heart (v. 26).
2. By bringing His great mercy to our mind.
3. By making us receive new mercy (vv. 28-30).
4. By revealing Himself and His methods of grace (v. 32).

- There are no arguments like those that are drawn from the consideration of the great and glorious things Christ has done for you; and if such will not take with you, and win upon you, I do not think the throwing of hell-fire in your faces will ever do it.   —Thomas Brooks

- Repentance—the tear dropped from the eye of faith.

- God's favor melts hard hearts sooner than the fire of His indignation; His kindness is very penetrative, it gets into the hearts of sinners sooner than His threats and frowns; it is like a small soaking rain, which goes to the roots of things, whereas a dashing rain runs away, and does little good. It was David's kindness that broke the heart of Saul (1 Sam. 24), and it's God's kindness which breaks the hearts of sinners.

- The milk and honey of the gospel affect the hearts of sinners more than the gall and wormwood of the law; Christ on Mount Zion brings more to repentance than Moses on Mount Sinai.
                                                        —William Greenhill

"Some people," says Philip Henry, "do not wish to hear much of repentance, but I think it so necessary that, if I should die in the pulpit, I wish to die preaching repentance; and if out of the pulpit, practicing it."

C.H. SPURGEON

A MAN TROUBLED BY HIS THOUGHTS

"His thoughts troubled him" (Daniel 5:6).

> To many men thinking is an unusual employment.
> Yet it is a distinction of man that he can think.
> No wonder that when thought is forced on some men they are troubled.

I. It Did Not Appear Likely That His Thoughts Would Trouble Him.

1. He was an irresponsible and reckless monarch.

2. He had hardened his heart with pride (vv. 22 and 23). Daniel said, "Thou hast lifted up thyself against the Lord of heaven."

3. He was drinking wine and it had worked upon him (v. 2)

4. He was celebrating in riotous company.

5. He was using profanity (v. 3)—daring to abuse the sacred vessels, in his banquets, as an expression of his contempt for Israel's God, Whom he despised.

> No man is rendered wise or thoughtful by the wine-cup.
> No man is out of the reach of the arrows of God.
> No conscience is so dead that God cannot arouse it.

II. Yet Well Might His Thoughts Trouble Him.

1. For what he saw was appalling: (v. 5).

2. For what he could not see was suggestive. Where was the hand? Where was the writer? What had he written? What did it mean?

3. For what he had done was alarming. His own past flashed before him. His cruel wars, oppressions, blasphemies and vices.

> What he had himself failed to do came before him (v. 23).
> What he was then in the act of doing startled him.

III. And Might Not Your Thoughts Trouble Some of You?

1. You are prosperous. Are not beasts fattened for the slaughter?

2. You are trifling with holy things. You neglect, or ridicule, or use without seriousness the things of God.

3. You mix with the impure. Will you not perish with them?

4. Your father's history might instruct you, or at least trouble you.

5. The sacred writing "over against the candlestick" is against you. Read the Holy Scripture, and see for yourself.

Conscience, from inaction is like a withered arm in the souls of many; but the Lord of conscience will one day say to it, "Be thou stretched forth, and do thine appointed work."

- As the ant-hill, when stirred, sets in motion its living insects in every direction, so the conscience of the sinner, disturbed by the Spirit, or judgments of God, calls up before its vision thousands of deeds which fill the soul with agony and woe.
—McCosh

The Duke of Wellington once said that he could have saved the lives of a thousand men a year, had he had chaplains or any religious ministers. The uneasiness of their minds reacted on their bodies, and kept up continual fever, once it seized upon their frames. It is our blessed office to tell of One Who can "minister to a mind diseased," Whose grace can deliver from "an evil conscience," and through Whom all inward fear and trouble are removed.

Charles IX, of France, in his youth, had humane and tender sensibilities. The fiend who had tempted him was the mother who had nursed him. When she first proposed to him the massacre of the Huguenots, he shrunk from it with horror: "No, no, madam! They are my loving subjects." Then was the critical hour of his life. Had he cherished that natural sensitiveness to bloodshed, St. Bartholomew's Eve would never have disgraced the history of his kingdom, and he himself would have escaped the fearful remorse which crazed him on his death-bed.

To his physician he said in his last hours, "Asleep or awake, I see the mangled forms of the Huguenots passing before me. They drip with blood. They make hideous faces at me. They point to their open wounds and mock me. Oh, that I had spared at least the little infants at the breast!" Then he broke out in agonizing cries and screams. Bloody sweat oozed from the pores of his skin.

- He was one of the few cases in history which confirm the possibility of the phenomenon which attended our Lord's anguish in Gethsemane. That was the fruit of resisting, years before, the recoil of his youthful conscience from the extreme of guilt.
—Austin Phelps
C.H. SPURGEON

THE STROKE OF THE CLOCK

"Sow to yourselves in righteousness, reap in mercy, break up your fallow ground: for it is time to seek the Lord, till He come and rain righteousness upon you" (Hosea 10:12).

What should we think of a farmer who allowed his finest field to lie fallow year after year? Yet men neglect their souls; and besides being unprofitable, these inward fields become full of weeds, and exceedingly foul.

I. **When Is It Time?** "It is time."

    1. In the very first hour of responsibility it is none too soon.

    2. At the present it is late, but not too late. "It is time."

    3. When chastening has come, seek the Lord instantly; for now it is high time, "lest a worse thing come unto thee" (John 5:14).

    4. Have you not sinned long enough? (1 Peter 4:3).

    5. When you assume great responsibilities, and enter on a new stage of life:—married, made a manager, a father, etc. (1 Chron. 22:19).

    6. When God's Spirit is specially at work and, therefore, others are saved (Acts 3:19).

II. **What Is the Particular Work?** "To seek the Lord."

    1. To draw nigh unto God; seeking Him in worship, prayer, etc. (Ps. 105:4).

    2. To ask pardon at His hands through the atonement of Jesus (Isa. 55:6).

    3. To obtain the blessings connected with the new birth (John 1:12, 13).

    4. To live for His glory: seeking His honor in all things (Matt. 6:33).
Suppose a pause between the seeking and the blessing, do not look in some other direction, but seek the Lord still.
What else can you do? (John 6:68).
It is sure to come. He will come, and will not tarry (Heb. 10:37).

III. **What Will Come of It?**

    1. He will come. God's coming in grace is all you need.

    2. He will come in abundance of grace meeting your obedient sowing. Mark the precept, "Sow in righteousness."

        Then note the promise, "and rain righteousness upon you."

    3. In consequence of the Lord's coming to you in righteousness, you shall "reap in mercy."

        Come then, and seek the Lord at this very hour! If you

would find Him, He is in Christ. Believe, and you have found Him, and righteousness in Him (Rom. 3:22).

Sir Thomas More, while he was a prisoner in the Tower, would not so much as suffer himself to be trimmed, saying that there was a controversy between the king and him for his head, and till that was at a happy end, he would be at no cost about it.

Let us but skim off the froth of his wit, and we may make a solemn use of it; for certainly all the cost we bestow upon ourselves, to make our lives pleasurable and joyous to us, is but mere folly, till it be decided what will become of the suit between God and us.

- It is said, "He who gets out of debt grows rich." Most sure it is that the pardoned soul cannot be poor; for as soon as peace is concluded, a free trade is opened between God and the soul. If once pardoned, we may then sail to any port that lies in God's dominions, and be welcome. All the promises stand open with their treasures, and say, "Here, poor soul, take in a full load of all precious things, even as much as your faith can bear and carry away!" —John Spencer

- A little maiden stood trembling, weeping, timidly knocking at the door of a minister's library. "Come in," said a cheerful voice. The door handle slowly turned, and there she stood, sobbing with emotion. "What is the matter, my dear child?" said the sympathetic pastor. "Oh, sir," was the reply, "I have lived seven years without Jesus!" She had just been celebrating her seventh birthday. —*The British Messenger*

Thomas Fuller says, "God invites many with His golden scepter whom He never bruises with His rod of iron." If the invitations of His grace were more freely accepted, we should often escape the chastisements of His hand.

Oh, that men did but know that a time of health, and happiness, and prosperity is as fit a season as can be for seeking the Lord! Indeed, any hour is a good time in which to seek the Lord, so long as it is present with us. He who would be wise will find no better day in the calendar for casting away folly than that which is not with him.

But let no man trifle with time, for in an instant the die may be cast, and then it is written concerning the ungodly, "I also will laugh at your calamity, and mock when your fear cometh" (Prov. 1:26).

C.H. SPURGEON

REST FOR THE RESTLESS

"Come unto Me, all ye that labor and are heavy laden, and I will give you rest."

"Take My yoke upon you, and learn of Me; for I am meek and lowly in heart; and ye shall find rest unto your souls. For My yoke is easy, and My burden is light" (Matthew 11:28-30).

Jesus had first taught the solemn truth of *human responsibility* (vv. 20-24), and afterwards He had joyfully proclaimed in prayer the doctrine of *election*: now He turns to give a free and full invitation to those who are needing rest. These three things are quite consistent, and should be found in all Christian preaching.

I. A Character Which Describes You.

1. Laboring, "all ye that labor," in whatever form.

In the service of formal religion, in attempt to keep the law, or in any other way of self-justification.

In the service of self to get gain, honor, ease, etc.

In the service of Satan, lust, drink, infidelity.

2. Laden. All who are "heavy laden," are called.

Laden with sin, guilt, dread, remorse, fear of death.

Laden with care, anxiety, greed, ambition, etc.

Laden with sorrow, poverty, oppression, slander, etc.

II. A Blessing Which Invites You.

1. Rest to be given. "I will give you rest."

To the conscience, by atonement and pardon.

To the mind, by infallible instruction and establishment.

To the heart a rest for love.

To the energies, by giving an object worth attaining.

To the apprehensions, assuring that all things work for good.

III. A Direction to Guide You.

1. *"Come* unto Me."

Come to a Person, to Jesus, the living Savior and Example.

Come at once, Jesus is ready now. Are you?

2. *"Take* My yoke upon you."

Be obedient to My command.

Be willing to be conformed to Me in service and burden bearing.

3. *"Learn* of Me."

You do not know; but must be content to learn.

You must not argue; but have a mind to learn.

You must learn by heart, and copy My meekness and lowliness.

- *"I will give you rest."* Rest for the burdened conscience, in pardon; for the unquiet intellect, in truth; for the aching, thirsty heart, in divine love; for the care-fretted spirit, in God's providence and promises; for the weary with sorrow and suffering, in the present foretaste, and shortly in the actual enjoyment of "His rest." —E.R. Conder

- "Come," says Christ, "and I will give you rest." I will not *show* you rest, nor barely *tell* you of rest, but I will *give* you rest. I am faithfulness itself, and cannot lie, I *will* give you rest. I who have the greatest power to give it, the greatest will to give it, the greatest right to give it, come, laden sinners, and *I* will give you rest.
Rest is the most desirable good, the most suitable good, and to you the greatest good. Come, says Christ; that is, believe in Me, and I will give you rest; I will give you peace with God, and peace with conscience: I will turn your storm into an everlasting calm; I will give you such rest, that the world can neither give to you nor take from you. —Thomas Brooks

- Lord, Thou madest us for Thyself, and we can find no rest till we find rest in Thee! —Augustine

- There are many heads resting on Christ's bosom, but there's room for yours there. —Samuel Rutherford
C.H. Spurgeon

It Never Comes

Many a stormcloud gathering o'er us
  Never comes to bring us rain;
Many a grief we see before us
  Never comes to give us pain.

Ofttimes in the feared tomorrow
  Sunshine comes, the cloud is gone;
Look not then in foolish sorrow
  For the trouble yet to come.
            —Author Unknown

CHOOSING THE WRONG

"But when the young man heard that saying, he went away sorrowful: for he had great possessions" (Matthew 19:22).

Introduction

Man is a free moral agent, he may choose either bad or good. This youth chose the worst.

I. The Rich Young Ruler's Choice.
1. He was a nice, clean-cut gentleman (Matt. 19:18, 20).
2. He made an effort to accept Christ.
3. The price was too great.
4. He turned away from Christ, thus choosing riches and sin.
5. We have no record of him ever coming again to Christ.

II. Choice Offered at the Trial of Christ (Matt. 27:16-22).
1. It was customary for the governor to release one prisoner of the Jews' choice on each feast day.
2. They had their minds made up in evil.
3. They made the evil choice of Barabbas (v. 20).
4. They chose crucifixion for Christ (v. 22).
5. The choice of anything instead of Christ is poor.
6. What stands between you and Christ today?

III. Felix Makes a Bad Choice (Acts 24:25).
1. Paul brought the Gospel to him.
2. Felix was moved by the power of the Gospel.
3. He must now make a choice for or against.
4. He chose to accept at a more convenient time.
5. You are about to decide with the man who made a bad choice.

IV. Agrippa Almost Persuaded to the Right (Acts 26:28).
1. He was moved by the Gospel.
2. He must make a decision.
3. He almost made the right choice but failed.
4. Almost will not prevail.
5. As far as we know this was his final decision.
6. You will make your last decision someday by merely failing to accept Christ.

JOHN C. JERNIGAN

THE BLIND BEGGAR OF JERICHO

"And Jesus stood still, and commanded him to be called. And they call the blind man, saying unto him, Be of good comfort, rise; he calleth thee. And he, casting away his garment, rose, and came to Jesus" (Mark 10:49,50).

This man is a picture of what we would hope every seeker of Christ might become.

In his lonely darkness, and deep poverty, he thought and became persuaded that Jesus was the Son of David.

Though he had no sight, he made good use of his hearing. If we have not all gifts, let us use those which we have.

I. He Sought the Lord Under Discouragements.

1. No one prompted his seeking.

2. Many opposed his attempts. "Many charged him that he should hold his peace" (v. 48).

3. For a while he was unheeded by the Lord Himself.

4. He was but a blind beggar, and this alone might have checked some pleaders.

II. He Received Encouragement.

This came from our Lord's commanding him to be called.

There are several kinds of calls which come to men at the bidding of our Lord Jesus. There is the—

1. Universal call. Jesus is lifted up that all who look to Him may live (John 3:14,15). The Gospel is preached to every creature.

2. Character call. To those who labor, and are heavy laden. Many are the Gospel promises which call the sinful, the mourning, the weary to Jesus (Isa. 55:7; Matt. 11:28; Acts 2:38,39).

3. Ministerial call. Given by the Lord's sent servants, and so backed by His authority (Acts 13:26, 38, 39; 16:31).

III. But Encouragement Did Not Content Him; He Still Sought Jesus.

To stop short of Jesus and healing would have been folly indeed.

1. He arose. Hopefully, resolutely, he quitted his begging posture. To receive salvation we must be on the alert, and in earnest.

2. He cast away his garment, and every hindrance. Our righteousness, our comfortable sin, our habit—anything, everything we must quit for Christ.

3. He came to Jesus. In the darkness occasioned by his blindness, he followed the Savior's voice.

4. He stated his case. "Lord, that I might receive my sight!"

5. He received salvation. Jesus said unto him, "Thy faith hath made thee whole." He obtained perfect eyesight; and in all respects he was in complete health.

IV. Having Found Jesus, He Kept Him.

1. He used his sight to see his Lord.
2. He became His avowed disciple. (See verse 52).
3. He went with Jesus on His way to the cross, and to the crown.
4. He remained a well-known disciple, whose father's name is given.

- *"And commanded him to be called."* By this circumstance he administered reproof and instruction: reproof, by ordering those to help the poor man who had endeavored to check him: instruction, by teaching us that, though He does not stand in need of our help, He will not dispense with our services; that we are to aid each other; that though we cannot recover our fellow-creatures, we may frequently bring them to the place and means of cure.   —William Jay

- Success in this world comes only to those who exhibit determination. Can we hope for salvation unless our mind is truly set upon it? Grace makes a man to be as resolved to be saved as this beggar was to get to Jesus, and gain his sight. "I must see him," said an applicant at the door of a public person. "You cannot see him," said the servant; but the man waited at the door. A friend went out to him, and said, "You cannot see the master, but I can give you an answer." "No," said the unfortunate pleader, "I will stay all night on the doorstep, but I will see the man himself. He alone will serve my turn."

    You do not wonder that, after many rebuffs, he ultimately gained his point: it would be an infinitely greater wonder if an importunate sinner did not obtain an audience from the Lord Jesus. If you must have grace, you shall have it. If you will not be put off, you shall not be put off. Whether things look favorable, or unfavorable, press on till you find Jesus, and you shall find Him.

                              —C.H. Spurgeon

LOVE'S FOREMOST

"Tell me, therefore, which of them will love him most?" (Luke 7:42).

I. We Must First Be Saved in the Same Manner as Others.

The road to eminence in love is just the plain way of salvation, which all who are in Christ must travel.

1. All are in debt; we must heartily own this to be our own case.

2. The loving Lord forgives in each case: personally we have exceeding great need of such remission. We must feel this.

3. In each case He forgives frankly, or without any consideration or compensation; it must be so with us. We must accept free grace and undeserved favor.

II. We Must Aim at a Deep Sense of Sin.

1. It was the *consciousness* of great indebtedness which created the great love in the penitent woman. Not her sin, but the consciousness of it was the basis of her loving character.

2. It is to be cultivated. The more we bewail sin the better, and we must aim at great tenderness of heart in reference to it. In order to cultivate it we must seek to get—

A clearer view of the law's requirements (Luke 10:26,27).

A deeper consciousness of the love of God to us (1 John 3:1,2).

A keener valuation of the cost of the redemption (1 Peter 1:18,19).

A surer persuasion of the perfection of our pardon will also help to show the baseness of our sin (Ezek. 16:62,63).

III. This Will Lead to a Highly Loving Conduct Toward Our Lord.

1. We shall desire to be near Him, even at His feet.

2. We shall show deep humility, delighting even to wash His feet.

3. We shall exhibit thorough contrition, beholding Him with tears.

4. We shall render earnest service; doing all that lies in our power for Jesus, even as this woman did.

A spiritual experience which is thoroughly flavored with a deep and bitter sense of sin is of great value to him who has had it. It is terrible in the drinking, but it is wholesome in the bowels, and in the whole of the after-life. Possibly much of the flimsy piety of the day arises from the ease with which men reach to peace and joy in these evangelistic days.

We would not judge modern converts, but we certainly prefer that form of spiritual exercise which leads the soul by the way of the Weeping-cross, and makes it see its blackness before it assures it that it is "clean every whit." Too many think lightly of sin and, therefore, lightly of a Savior.

He who has stood before His God, convicted, and condemned, with the rope about his neck, is the man to weep for joy when he is pardoned, to hate the evil which has been forgiven him, and to live to the honor of the Redeemer by Whose Blood he has been cleansed.

Bold blasphemers ought to be enthusiasts for the honor of their Lord when they are washed from their iniquities. As they say, reclaimed poachers make the best game-keepers, so should the greatest sinners be the raw material out of which the Lord's transforming grace shall create great saints.

- I have heard say the depth of a Scotch lake corresponds with the height of the surrounding mountains. So deep thy sense of obligation for pardoned sin, so high thy love to Him Who has forgiven thee.   —C.H.S.

- Love to the Savior rises in the heart of a saved man in proportion to the sense which he entertains of his own sinfulness on the one hand, and of the mercy of God on the other. Thus the height of a saint's love to the Lord is as the depths of his own humility: as this root strikes down unseen into the ground, the blossoming branch rises higher in the sky.   —William Arnot
C.H. SPURGEON

What's Happened to Love?

About 200 years ago a well-known encyclopedia discussed the word "atom" with the use of only four lines. But five pages were devoted to a discussion of "love."

In a recent edition of the same encyclopedia five pages were given to the word "atom"; "love" was omitted.

PUTTING CHRIST LAST

"And he said unto another, Follow me. But he said, Lord, suffer me first to go and bury my father. And another also said, Lord, I will follow thee; but let me first go bid them farewell, which are at home at my house" (Luke 9:59, 61).

Introduction
The Church and world too often put Christ last.

    I. **Christ Said to a Man, "Follow Me."**
       1. The man made no special objections.
       2. He seemed to be willing.
       3. But he wanted to bury his father first.

    II. **Another Said, "I Will Follow Thee."**
       1. He seemed to be anxious.
       2. His statement was volunteered.
       3. His home folks came before Christ.
       4. He would follow Christ if he could let his people come first.

    III. **Church Members Often Put Him Last.**
       1. I will do this for my people, and then for the Church.
       2. I will pay for my car and then pay tithes.
       3. After I get out of debt I will help some then.
       4. When I get more time I want to pray more.
       5. I would like to attend church but have so much to do.
       6. You have put Christ last.

    IV. **Sinners Put Christ Last.**
       1. I am young and have plenty of time.
       2. Would like to enjoy the pleasures of sin a while longer.
       3. Would like to make more money before I start.
       4. I fear what my friends would say about me.

    V. **Those Who Have Put Christ Last.**
       1. Are not fit for the kingdom of God (Luke 9:62).
       2. How would you like to meet Him in judgment after you have put Him last? He will put you last.
       3. God is a jealous God (Ex. 20:5). He must be first.

Conclusion
Put the one first you love best. That is the way your love is measured. How much do you love God?   JOHN C. JERNIGAN

HE RAN, AND HE RAN

"But when he saw Jesus afar off, he ran and worshiped Him" (Mark 5:6). *"But when he was yet a great way off, his father saw him, and had compassion, and ran . . . and kissed him"* (Luke 15:20).

These two texts have a measure of apparent likeness: the man runs to Jesus from afar, and the Father runs to the prodigal from afar.

I. The Sinner's Place. "Afar off."

Jesus is afar off in the sinner's apprehension.

1. As to *character*. What a difference between the demoniac and the Lord Jesus: between the prodigal son and the great Father!

2. As to *knowledge*. The demoniac knew Jesus but knew little of His love. The prodigal knew little of his Father's great heart.

3. As to *possession*. The demoniac had no hold upon the Savior; on the contrary he cried, "What have I to do with Thee?" The prodigal thought he had lost all claim to his Father, and therefore said, "I am no more worthy to be called Thy son."

Immeasurable is the distance between God and a sinner.

II. The Sinner's Privilege. "He saw Jesus."

This much you, who are most under Satan's influence, are able to see concerning Jesus: you know that—

1. There is such a Person. He is God and Man, the Savior.
2. He has done great things.
3. He is able to cast out the powers of evil.
4. He may cast them out from you, and deliver you.

III. The Secret of Hope for Sinners. "His father saw him."

1. The returning sinner was seen from afar by Omniscience.
2. He was recognized as a son is known by his Father.
3. He was understood, beloved, and accepted by his Father.

- God will pardon a repentant sinner more quickly than a mother would snatch her child out of the fire.   —Vianney

A soul in distress runs to Jesus: God in compassion runs to meet returning wanderers. With sin within you, Christ before you, time pressing you, eternity awaiting you, hell beneath you, heaven above you; O sinner, you may indeed well run! He that would have heaven must run for it.

C.H. SPURGEON

THE PRODIGAL SON

"Bring hither the fatted calf, and kill it; and let us eat and be merry. For this my son was dead, and is alive again; he was lost, and is found" (Luke 15:23,24).

The willingness of God to receive sinners is abundantly declared in Scripture, but in no place is it so amply, or so beautifully described as in the parable before us.

The reference which the parable has to the Jews and Gentiles will be more properly noticed, when we come to consider the conduct of the elder brother. At present we may view it as a lively representation of a sinner's return to God.

The text calls our attention to three points (which are also the three distinguishing parts of the parable) namely, the prodigal's departure from his father, his return to him, and his reception with him.

I. His Departure.

He went from his father's house, little thinking of the ruin he should bring upon himself.

The *occasion* of his departure was, that he hated the restraint of his father's presence and longed for independence, that he might gratify his own inclinations. Thus he desired his father to divide him his portion, but little did he think to what *extent* his passions would carry him. Scarcely had he received his portion before he left his father and departed to a distant country, where his actions would pass unnoticed. Having thus surrendered himself to his appetites, he was carried on with irresistible impetuosity. From one degree of sin to another he rushed forward without restraint nor did he stop till he had wasted his substance in riotous living.

At last he began to feel the *consequences* of his folly. He was reduced to a state of extreme wretchedness, yet he determined to do any thing rather than return to his father. Though a Jew, he submitted for hire to the ignominious employment of feeding swine. His wages, however, there being a grievous famine in the land, would not procure him even necessary subsistence.

In vain did he attempt to fill his belly with the husks intended for the swine. In vain did he solicit assistance from those who had known him in his more prosperous days. "No man," either from gratitude or compassion, "gave him" any relief.

Such is the departure of sinners from the presence of their God. They have experienced the restraints of education, but have sighed for liberty and independence. With their growing years, they increasingly abuse the mercies which God has bestowed upon them. Their reason, their time, and other talents they employ in the service of sin. Though they do not all run to the same excess of riot, they live equally at a distance from God.

At last perhaps they begin to feel the misery which their neglect of Him has brought upon them. His providence too concurs with His grace to make a deeper wound in their conscience. But they try any carnal expedients rather than return to God, nor can they ever be prevailed upon to turn unto Him, till they have fully proved the insufficiency of the creature to afford them help.

Whatever they may think of themselves in such a state, they are really *"dead,"* and *"lost"*—but the prodigal was not gone beyond recovery, as is evident from,

II. His Return.

During his departure he had been as a person destitute of reason. At last however, *"coming to himself,"* he thought of his father's house.

The various steps of his return are worthy of notice. He first reflected on the folly and madness of his former ways and on the incomparably happier state of those who lived under his father's roof, and whom perhaps he once despised for submitting to such restraints. He then resolved that he would return to his father, and implore his forgiveness.

Having formed the purpose, he instantly arose to carry it into execution.

Destitute as he was, he set off to obtain, if possible, the lowest office among his father's servants. These exactly describe the steps of a sinner's return to God: He first begins to see how madly and wickedly he has acted. He feels that he has reduced himself to a wretched and perishing condition. He considers how happy are those once despised people, who enjoy the favor of his heavenly father, and how happy he himself should be, if he might but obtain the meanest place in his family.

With these views he determines to abase himself as a vile, self-ruined creature. There are no terms so humiliating, but he finds them suited to his case. He is rather fearful of not humbling himself sufficiently than of aggravating his sin too much. He resolves that he will go to a throne of grace and ask for mercy. Nor will he wait for any more convenient season, lest he should perish before the hoped-for season arrived. He is ashamed indeed to go in so mean and destitute a condition, but he despairs of ever going in any other way. He, therefore, breaks through all the engagements he has made with sin and Satan and goes, with all his guilt upon him, to his God and Savior. He now perhaps may be deemed *mad* by his former companions but he should rather be considered as now *"coming to himself."* The effect of the prodigal's repentance appears in

III. His Reception.

His father, it seems, was watching hopefully for his return. On his first appearance, his father ran to show his good will toward him. The sight of the returning son caused the father to yearn over him, nor would he suffer an upbraiding word to escape his lips. When the prodigal began his confession, the father interrupted him with kisses, and not only would not hear the whole of his confession, but he would not even hurt his feelings by saying that he pardoned him. He ordered the best robe, with shoes and a ring, to be instantly put upon him, and killed the fatted calf in order to celebrate the joyful occasion.

What a delightful representation does this give us of the reception which penitents find with God! God longs for their salvation even while they are at a distance from Him. He notices with joy the first approaches of their souls toward Him. Instead of frowning on the prodigal, he received him with joy. Instead of upbraiding him with his folly, he seals upon his soul a sense of pardon. He arrays him in robes of righteousness and garments of salvation. He adorns him in a manner suited to the relation into which he is brought. He provides for his future comfortable and upright conversation. He rejoices over him as recovered from the dead, and makes it an occasion of festivity to all the angels in heaven.

Thus do even the vilest sinners find their hopes, not only realized, but far exceeded. They come for pardon, and obtain joy; for deliverance from hell, and get a title to heaven. Their utmost ambition is to be regarded as the meanest of God's servants: and they are exalted to all the honors and happiness of his beloved children.

CHARLES SIMEON

WHAT DOES IT MEAN TO BE LOST?

*"For the Son of man is come to seek and to save that which was lost"
(Luke 19:10).*

The child of God may be lost from fellowship with God and needs
to be found; but it is a different thing for a soul to be lost in the
sense that it needs to be saved. In Luke 15:4 we are told that Christ
goes out after the sheep until He finds it; but this must not be
confused with the words of our text, "For the Son of man is come to
seek and to save that which was lost."

I. **Every Individual Born into This World Inherits the Fallen
Nature of Adam.**

This is called the doctrine of total depravity. This doctrine is
not understood by man. It means that people are depraved in that
they can do nothing which is acceptable unto God.

This condition described by the words, "dead in trespasses and
sins," is that the spirit and soul of man are separated from God and
are helpless to return to God. The Bible is emphatic when stating
the truth that the unsaved, left to their own volition, will not turn to
God.

The individual may not be depraved because of his own sin any
more than he is responsible for his own ignorance in being born in
the world. But he must be saved.

II. **Men Are Deathbound Because of Sin.**

Here again the individual is not responsible. The Bible gives
just one reason for this "deathbound." It is because of the sin of
Adam.

It must be discerned that the judgment of death which fell
upon Adam and his posterity is not physical death alone; it included
both spiritual death and the "second" death.

III. **Judgment Rests Now Upon Men.**

This is because God has made a decree which reaches to all
men of this age. This decree declares that all unsaved people are
"under sin."

It is not difficult to see that to be under sin is a specific judgment
from God which is peculiar to the present age; for in no other age has
it ever been true that "there is no difference between Jew and Gentile."

All men are under sin until they are saved by grace. God is now calling both Jew and Gentile. Both must go through the same saving process.

IV. Men Are Lost Because of Sins They Have Committed.

The Scriptures declare that all have sinned and that there is none righteous. The first sin of Adam was an indifference to the demands of God. We commit sins in the same careless way. There is a vast difference between God's conception of sin and man's. But God has the twofold cure. He freely forgives and He freely justifies.

V. Men Are Lost Because They Are in the Power of Satan.

Not only is salvation of such a supernatural character that no human being could ever hope to accomplish it for himself, but all that enters in his lost condition can be remedied by God alone, and even God can undertake the salvation of a soul only as He is rendered free to do so through the death of Christ for that soul.

LEWIS S. CHAFER

Thoreau's Ignorance

When Thoreau, the naturalist, was close to death, he was visited by a very pious aunt who asked, "Henry, have you made your peace with God?" "I didn't know," was Thoreau's answer, "that we had ever quarreled."

And in his answer he revealed his profound spiritual ignorance. Too many people are like him. They are utterly unconscious of the fact that they have sinned against God and so have "quarreled" with Him, and are really lost and separated from God. The first step in coming to Christ is to realize one is a sinner, a lost sinner.

Thoreau's answer revealed that he still was a lost man: he didn't know he was lost and so he had never come to Christ to be saved. Here is a truth about man's sin and lost condition by nature that has not changed since Thoreau's time.

THE PENITENT THIEF

"But the other answering, rebuked him, saying, Dost not thou fear God, seeing thou art in the same condemnation? And we indeed justly; for we receive the due reward of our deeds: but this man hath done nothing amiss. And he said unto Jesus, Lord, remember me when thou comest into thy kingdom. And Jesus said unto him, Verily I say unto thee, today shalt thou be with me in paradise" (Luke 23:40-43).

Christ is said to have triumphed over principalities and powers on His cross, and surely the conversion and salvation of this poor sinner affords a wonderful instance of it, and serves as a specimen of His mercy to future ages. Well may it be said, "This is a faithful saying, and worthy of all acceptation, that Christ Jesus came into the world to save sinners, even the chief."

This unhappy man and his fellow sufferer were "malefactors," common thieves or robbers. They had probably been partners in crime, and both suffered for the same offense: but how great the difference between them in the final hour. The one dies in his impenitence, the other owns that he suffered justly, though at first they both railed on the dying Savior. We may, therefore, well consider the penitent thief as a singular instance of the power and grace of God toward the very chief of sinners. While falling himself a sacrifice to the malice of Satan, Jesus snatches a lamb as it were out of the mouth of the lion, and takes with him to paradise, a sinner who was sinking into the pit of destruction.

I. The Dying Thief Had Genuine Repentance.

His situation allowed him no other opportunity of showing his grief and sorrow for sin, than by the few words which dropped from his lips while he was suspended on the cross; but these afford full proof of his sincerity. His hands and feet were nailed, but his heart was free; and his lips not being yet closed in death, he will do all he can to glorify the Savior.

1. He begins to *rebuke* the reviling thief: "Dost not thou fear God?" His was genuine repentance, and genuine love, which could not bear that Jesus should be dishonored by railing accusations, nor that scandals should be cast on Him.

2. He *confesses his sin*, and acknowledges the equity of his sentence. "We indeed," says he, "suffer justly." His confession was public and open, in the presence of innumerable witnesses, and of

innumerable enemies. He had nothing to hope for from man, no prospect of deliverance. He was looking to Christ for salvation, but he owns his condemnation to be just. This indeed is confessing and giving glory to God, and that in the first place, and in the highest sense; for this confession was made *before* any plea for mercy was offered, so that whether he was saved or not, he justifies and glorifies God; and this is the spirit of genuine repentance.

3. He *vindicates* the character of Christ, while he unequivocally condemns himself. "This man has done nothing amiss." Herein indeed he charged his country with the guilt of crucifying the Lord of glory; and while he himself pleads guilty, he pleads the innocence of Christ before the same tribunal.

4. His repentance is accompanied with *faith in Christ*: he called Him "Lord." Multitudes were deriding Him, His disciples had all forsaken Him, and He was sinking under weakness and disgrace; yet this poor sinner owns Him as the Lord, a name which implies every high idea of Christ (1 Cor. 12:3). He also believes that Christ has a "kingdom," a kingdom not of this world, and that He was going to possess it. Though He now appeared as an outcast from heaven and earth, yet he considered Him as the Lord of the invisible world.

This was great faith, especially if we consider how this poor sinner came by the knowledge of Christ. Probably he could not read, was unacquainted with the prophecies, had never seen Jesus before, nor heard any thing about Him; His enemies triumphed, His friends were scattered. What he hears is only from the mouth of His accusers, and he had to collect his knowledge of Christ from the derision and scorn of the multitude.

5. His repentance is accompanied with *earnest prayer*: "Lord, remember me." This is very brief, but full and comprehensive, being the utterance of the heart. He does not specify the object of his prayer, yet he selects the most appropriate terms in which to express himself, and leaves it with the Lord to give him what he needed. He might have said, Lord, pardon me, bless me, and save me; but this includes all. "Let Me but have a place in your heart, and all the rest will follow." "*Lord*, remember me." He might have thought his sin too great to be pardoned, but he does not, neither does he despair of an interest in the Savior's love: Lord, remember *me*. Self-righteous pride would have prevented his making such an application for mercy as utterly in vain, and such a spirit would have objected to prayer on account of his utter unworthiness: but he is not discouraged by the greatness of his guilt.

II. "Verily I Say Unto Thee, Today Shalt Thou Be with Me in Paradise."

1. Though Christ would take no notice of a reviler, nor give any answer to the language of reproach, yet He would *attend to the plea of mercy*; and to the plea of one of the most unworthy, and the least likely to obtain it. He would hear the prayer of a perishing sinner whose heart was contrite, even in the hour of death. What condescension, and what love!

2. He answered him *without delay*. He for a time deferred the request of one poor woman who sought Him with great importunity, and suffered her to be repulsed; and though He answered at last, yet He kept her in long suspense (Matt. 15:22,23). But his was an urgent case: the sinner was dying, and the Savior so near at hand.

3. As the petition had *implied much*, so did the answer. To be with Jesus, to be with Him in paradise, was more than he could ask or think. This would be all in all, not only including the forgiveness of sin, acceptance with God, and eternal life, but more than could enter into the heart of man to conceive. The penitent had only asked of Jesus to *remember* him; but Jesus tells him he should be *with* Him. He asked to be remembered at some future time, he knew not when; but Jesus tells him that "today" he should be blessed.

4. The promise is pronounced with a solemn *assertion*; "Verily, I say unto thee." This bears the form of an oath, and gives the fullest assurance for the performance of the promise (Heb. 6:18).

Reflections:

1. We may observe that there is a great difference between the conduct of this dying thief and that of many dying penitents who are supposed to be converted. They often speak confidently of their state, and of their going to heaven; but this poor man did not, though Christ said so of him. He prayed that he might be saved; and after what Christ said, he might believe that he should; but he himself said not a word of that. The strong language that was used was Christ's, and not his.

2. The mercy shown to the penitent thief affords an encouraging example to perishing sinners.

3. There is a request on Christ's part as well as on ours: He desires to be remembered by us (1 Cor. 11:24). He does not need it as we do but love desires it, and wishes to live in the mind of its objects: CHARLES SIMEON

THE DOOR

"I am the door: by Me if any man enter in, he shall be saved, and shall go in and out, and find pasture" (John 10:9).

Our Lord sets Himself forth very condescendingly. The most sublime and poetical figures are none too glorious to describe Him; but He chooses homely ones, which the most prosaic minds can apprehend. A door is a common object. Jesus would have us often think of Him. A door to a sheepfold is the poorest form of door. Jesus condescends to be anything, so that He may serve and save His people.

I. The Door. In this homely illustration we see—

1. *Necessity.* Suppose there had been none, we could never have entered in to God, peace, truth, salvation, purity, or heaven.

2. *Singularity.* There is only one door; let us not weary ourselves to find another. Salvation is by entrance at that door, and at none other (Acts 4:12).

3. *Personality.* The Lord Jesus is Himself the door. "I am the door," saith He; not ceremonies, doctrines, professions, achievements, but the Lord Himself, our Sacrifice.

II. The Users of It.

1. They are not mere observers, or knockers at the door, or sitters down before it, or guards marching to and fro in front of it. But they *enter in* by faith, love, experience, communion.

2. They are persons who have the one qualification: they do *"enter in."* The person is "any man," but the essential distinction is entrance.

A door which is conspicuously marked as The Door is evidently meant to be used. The remarkable advertisement of "I am the door," and the special promises appended to it, are the most liberal invitation imaginable.

III. The Privileges of These Users.

1. *Salvation.* "He shall be saved." At once, forever, altogether.

2. *Liberty.* He "shall go in and out." This is no prison-door, but a door for a flock whose Shepherd gives freedom.

3. *Access.* "Shall go in," for pleading, hiding, fellowship, instruction, enjoyment.

4. *Egress.* "He shall go out," for service, progress, etc.

5. *Nourishment*. "And find pasture." Our spiritual food is found through Christ, in Christ, and around Christ.

- The work of the Reformation was thus described by Stern, a German statesman: "Thank heaven, Dr. Luther has made the entrance into heaven somewhat shorter, by dismissing a crowd of door-keepers, chamberlains, and masters of ceremony."

  —John Bate

- We cannot go abroad or return home without passing through an emblem of our Lord. So near as He is in the type, so near let Him be in reality. —C.H.S.

- There are not half-a-dozen ways out of our sin and misery— not a choice of ways over the steep hills and desolate waste- places of this mortal life, so that by any of them we may reach heaven at last, but only one way.

  But, if this is the only way, it is likewise a perfectly secure way. *Via unica, via certa*, is a Latin proverb in which the truth is stated very forcibly. —Dean Howson

  C.H. SPURGEON

Rescue of the "Squalas"

The submarine *Squalas* and its crew lay helpless at the bottom of the Atlantic Ocean, two hundred and forty feet below the surface. The crew sent up smoke flares, hoping that their location would become known.

A ten-ton diving bell was lowered several times, bringing to safety the thirty-three surviving members of the crew of the ill-fated *Squalas*.

Not one of the thirty-three men said to their rescuers, "I will think it over," or "I will wait for a more convenient season," or "I am in good condition as I am," or "There is too much to give up," or "I won't under- stand it until tomorrow." All instantly and gratefully accepted the means of escape from death.

—Robert G. Lee

HOW TO BECOME A CHRISTIAN

"Now when they heard this, they were pricked in their heart, and said unto Peter and to the rest of the apostles, Men and brethren, what shall we do? Then Peter said unto them, Repent, and be baptized every one of you in the name of Jesus Christ for the remission of sins, and ye shall receive the gift of the Holy Ghost" (Acts 2:37,38).

Introduction
The inquirers were sinners and wanted to become Christians. They asked how they might become Christians, and Peter answered their question.

- I. **One Must Believe That God Is (Heb. 11:6).**
    1. That is, believe there is a God.
    2. Believe that He will reward a sinner, forgive him.
    3. One must believe the Bible is God's Word.
    4. These inquiring Jews believed in God and the Bible.

- II. **One Must Be Convicted of His Sins.**
    1. The Holy Ghost convicts of sin (John 16:7,8).
    2. God draws men toward Christ (John 6:44).
    3. The inquiring Jews were deadly convicted.
    4. The Gospel had reached their hearts.
    5. God had spoken to them by the Gospel and Spirit.

- III. **Repentance Is the Next Step.**
    1. Except you repent you shall perish (Luke 13:3).
    2. Repentance is a command of God (Acts 17:30).
    3. John demanded it of his converts (Matt. 3:5-8).
    4. Christ preached on the subject of "Repentance" (Mark 1:15).

- IV. **Accept Christ by Faith.**
    1. Must by faith accept the free gift.
    2. If offered a gift, you would not receive it unless you accepted it.
    3. Christ offers pardon after you have met conditions, but you must accept to receive.

- V. **God's Part in Our Redemption.**
    1. To provide the atonement. He did in Christ.
    2. To convict or draw the sinner. This He is doing.
    3. When you fully decide, confessing your sins in faith, He will forgive (1 John 1:9).

Conclusion
Why be lost? God will do all of His part and help you to do yours.

JOHN C. JERNIGAN

"TO YOU"

"To you is the word of this salvation sent" (Acts 13:26).

I. What Is the Word of This Salvation?

1. It is the testimony that Jesus is the promised Savior (v. 23).

2. The word which promises forgiveness to all who exhibit repentance of sin, and faith in the Lord Jesus (vv. 38,39).

3. In a word, it is the proclamation of perfect salvation, through the risen Savior (vv. 32,33).

It is a word of *salvation*; for it declares, describes, presents, and presses home salvation.

It is a word *sent*, for the Gospel dispensation is a mission of mercy from God, the Gospel is a message, Jesus is the Messiah, and the Holy Ghost Himself is *sent* to work salvation among men.

II. In What Manner Is the Gospel Sent to You?

1. In the general commission, which ordains that it be preached to every creature.

2. In the providence which has brought you this day to hear the Word.

3. In the peculiar adaptation of it to your case, character, and necessity. A medicine which suits your disease is evidently meant for you.

It would be a sad thing if we had to single out even one, and say, "This word is *not* sent to you."

III. In What Position Does It Place You?

1. Of singular favor. Prophets and kings died without hearing what you hear (Matt. 13:16).

2. Of notable indebtedness to martyrs and men of God, in the past ages, and in these days; for these have lived and died to bring you the Gospel.

3. Of great hopefulness; for we trust you will accept it and live.

4. Of serious responsibility; for if you neglect it, how will you escape? (Heb. 2:3).

IV. In What Manner Will You Treat This Word?

1. Will you basely and foolishly delay your reply? This is a very dangerous course, and many perish in it.

2. Will you play the hypocrite, and pretend to receive it, while in your heart you reject it?

3. Will you act the part of the temporary convert?
4. Will you not rather accept the word of salvation with delight?
Jesus said, "Preach the Gospel to every creature." I can imagine Peter was asking Him: "What, Lord! shall we offer salvation to the men who crucified You?" And I imagine Jesus answering him: "Yes, Peter, I want you to preach My Gospel to everybody, beginning at Jerusalem. Proclaim salvation to the men who crucified Me.

- "Peter, I'd like you to find that man who put the crown of thorns on My head. Tell him, if he'll take salvation as a gift, he shall have a crown of glory from Me, and there sha'nt be a thorn in it. Look up that Roman soldier who thrust that spear into My side, to My very heart, and tell him that there's a nearer way to My heart than that. My heart is full of love for his soul. Proclaim salvation to him." —D.L. Moody

- *To whom* is it that the God of salvation sent "the word of salvation"? He sent it to all sinners that hear it. It is a word that suits the case of sinners; and, therefore, it is sent to them. If it be inquired, for what *purpose* is it sent to sinners? . . . It is sent as a word of *pardon* to the condemned sinner. Hence may every condemned sinner take hold of it, saying, This word is sent to me. It is sent as a word of *peace* to the rebellious sinner.

   It is sent as a word of *life* to the dead. It is a word of *liberty* to the captives, of *healing* for the diseased, of *cleansing* to the polluted. It is a word of *direction* to the bewildered, and of *refreshment* to the weary. It is sent as a *comforting* word to the disconsolate; and as a *drawing* word and a *strengthening* word to the soul destitute of strength. It is sent, in short, as a *word of salvation*, and *all sorts* of salvation and redemption to the lost soul, saying, "Christ came to seek and to save that which was lost." —*Condensed from* Ralph Erskine
C.H. SPURGEON

JUSTIFICATION BY FAITH

"We conclude that a man is justified by faith without the deeds of the law" (Romans 3:28).

These words contain a conclusion drawn from the principles laid down in the preceding context, which we must examine, if we would understand and feel the force of the inference. Having expressed this readiness to preach the Gospel at Rome, St. Paul proceeded to show the need which all have of the Gospel, the "wrath of God being revealed against all unrighteousness and ungodliness of men," and to point out the wickedness and inexcusableness of the Gentiles, and also of the Jews, in evidence of which he alleges the testimony of their own inspired writers, David and Solomon, in the best ages of their church. Hence all being sinners, and involved in guilt and condemnation, and therefore, incapable of being justified by the law, God has appointed another way of justification; we say a man is "justified by faith without the deeds of the law."

I. What Is Meant by Justification.

The justification here meant is not that which comes upon all men, even infants, through the righteousness of Christ, Romans 5:14,15, 18. It is not that which shall take place at the day of judgment, spoken of, Romans 2:13-16, and by our Lord, Matthew 12:37, which will be, not indeed by the merit, Romans 6:23, but by the evidence of works. Revelation 20:12; 22:12. It is the justification, which the true people of God experience, and possess on earth; 1 Corinthians 6:11; Titus 3:7; which is—not the being acquitted of all blame, or declared to be innocent, which is the meaning of the word "justified," in courts of law: Psalms 143:2; 3:20:—not the being made innocent, or holy, or righteous, which would confound it with regeneration or sanctification:—But having righteousness accounted, or imputed, to us, sin not imputed, sin pardoned, or the sentence of condemnation gone out against us reversed. This is our obligation to punishment canceled, and this by a judicial act of God.

II. In What Sense Are We to Be "Justified by Faith"?

When the Apostle says, we are "justified by faith," he does not speak of the *moving cause* of justification, which is the divine love, mercy, or grace; and hence we are said to be justified by grace; v. 24; Titus 3:4-7: nor of the *meritorious cause*, which is the redemption of Christ; vv. 24,25; Isaiah 53:11; 2 Corinthians 5 *ult.*; and hence we are said to be "justified by Christ; Galatians 2:17;—nor of the *efficient cause*, either of the preparation necessary, as conviction and repentance for sin, or of a sense of this justification; this is the Holy Spirit, and may be meant, Titus 3:7:—nor of the *instrumental cause on the part of* God, which is His Word, viz. His declarations and promises respecting pardoning the penitent: of this our Lord speaks, John 15:3:—But of the *instrumental cause on our part*, which is faith—in Christ, as the Son of God, the Messiah, the Savior, able and willing to save: John 3:16-18; Galatians 2:16; this implies that we come to Him; John 6:37; 7:37; Matthew 11:28; that we trust in Him, as "delivered for our offenses," Romans 4:25, trust in His blood, Romans 3:25, and that we receive Him, John 1:12,—in God, Romans 4:24,—in His mercy and promises through Christ, Romans 4:17-23.

III. How This Is "Without the Deeds of the Law."

The law meant here, is chiefly the moral law, Romans 2:17,18, 21-23, 25. The sins mentioned in this chapter, vv. 10, 18, are all breaches of the moral law; it is this also which is meant, Romans 7. The deeds of this law are the obedience required in it, viz. in the Ten Commandments, or in those two respecting love to God and our neighbor, because they cannot precede it, we neither do, nor can do them till we are justified; then only do we begin to love and serve a pardoning God. But how does this consist with St. James' doctrine? Romans 2:14-26. Abraham was justified years before Isaac was born, but his offering him up at God's command, showed the reality and power of his faith, that it wrought by love, a love to God greater than to Isaac. Thus it declared and evidenced his faith. So was Rahab's faith evidenced, and in this way our faith must be made manifest; for the works of the law must follow our justification. Our faith must "work," Galatians 5:6; 1 Thessalonians 1:3; the law must be "established," v. 31, and its "righteousness fulfilled in us," by love, Romans 8:3,4; 13:10; Galatians 5:14. We must make the law a rule of life, must view ourselves in it as in a glass, that we may see our great deficiency, and be kept in an humble disposition; must consider it as holding out to our view that "holiness without which no man shall see the Lord." But our obedience to the law can never merit our acceptance even after our justification; we can claim this and eternal life solely on the ground of justification through Christ's merits. No one penitent need despair on account of his sins—no one should presume on account of his righteousness. If we be justified by faith, we may be justified *now*.   CHARLES SIMEON

BOUGHT WITH A PRICE

"And ye are not your own, for ye are bought with a price: therefore glorify God in your body, and in your spirit; which are God's" (1 Corinthians 6:19,20).

With what ardor does the apostle pursue sin to destroy it! He is not so prudish as to let sin alone, but cries out, in plainest language, "Flee fornication." The shame is not in the rebuke, but in the sin which calls for it.

He chases this foul wickedness with arguments (see v. 18).

He drags it into the light of the Spirit of God. "What? Know ye not that your body is the temple of the Holy Ghost?" (v. 19).

He slays it at the cross. "Ye are bought with a price."

Let us consider the last argument, that we may find therein death for our sins.

I. A Blessed Fact. "Ye are brought with a price."

"Ye are bought." This is that idea of Redemption which modern heretics dare to style *mercantile*. The mercantile redemption is the Scriptural one; for the expression, "bought with a price," is a double declaration of that idea.

1. This is either a fact or not. "Ye are brought, or ye are unredeemed." Terrible alternative.

2. If a fact, it is *the* fact of your life. A wonder of wonders.

3. It will remain to you eternally the greatest of all facts. If true at all, it will never cease to be true, and it will never be outdone in importance by any other event.

4. It should, therefore, operate powerfully upon us both now and ever.

II. A Plain Consequence. "Ye are not your own."

Negative. It is clear that if bought, ye are *not* your own.

1. This involves privilege.

You are not your own provider: sheep are fed by their shepherd.

You are not your own guide: ships are steered by their pilot.

2. This also involves responsibility.

We are not our own to injure. Neither body nor soul.

Not our own to waste, in idleness, amusement, or speculation.

Not our own to exercise caprice, and follow our own prejudices, depraved affections, wayward wills, or irregular appetites. *Positive.* "Your body and your spirit, which are God's."

We are altogether God's. Body and spirit include the whole man.

We are always God's. The price once paid, we are forever His.

III. A Practical Conclusion. "Glorify God in your body, and in your spirit, which are God's."

Glorify God *in your body*.

By cleanliness, chastity, temperance, industry, cheerfulness, self-denial, patience, etc.

Glorify God—

In a suffering body by patience unto death.

In a working body by holy diligence.

In a worshiping body by bowing in prayer.

In a well-governed body by self-denial.

In an obedient body by doing the Lord's will with delight.

Glorify God *in your spirit*.

By holiness, faith, zeal, love, heavenliness, cheerfulness, fervor, humility, expectancy, etc.

- But why should so vast a price be required? Is man worth the cost? A man may be bought in parts of the world for the value of an ox. It was not man simply, but man in a certain relation, that had to be redeemed. See one who has been all his days a drunken, idle, worthless fellow. All appropriate to him the epiphet "worthless"—worth nothing.

But that man commits a crime for which he is sentenced to be hanged, or to be imprisoned for life. Go and try to buy him now. Redeem him and make him your servant. Let the richest man in Cambridge offer every shilling he possesses for that worthless man, and his offer would be wholly vain, why? Because now there is not only the man to be considered, but the law. It needs a very great price to redeem one man from the curse of the law of England; but Christ came to redeem all men from the curse of the Divine law.   —William Robinson
C.H. SPURGEON

SORROW AND SORROW

"For godly sorrow worketh repentance to salvation not to be repented of: but the sorrow of the world worketh death" (2 Corinthians 7:10).

Time was when inner experience was considered to be everything, and experimental preaching was the order of the day.
Sinners were unwisely influenced by certain ministries to look to their own feelings; and many began to seek comfort from their own misery.
Now it is "only believe." And rightly so: but we must discriminate.
There must be sorrow for sin working repentance.

I. **Remove Certain Erroneous Ideas with Regard to Repentance and Sorrow for Sin.**
   Among popular delusions we must mention the suppositions—
   1. That mere sorrow of mind in reference to sin is repentance.
   2. That there can be repentance without sorrow for sin.
   3. That we must reach a certain point of wretchedness and horror, or else we are not truly penitent.
   4. That repentance happens to us once, and is then over.

II. **Distinguish Between the Two Sorrows Mentioned in the Text.**
   1. The godly sorrow which worketh repentance to salvation is—
      Sorrow for sin as committed against God.
      Sorrow for sin arising out of an entire change of mind.
      Sorrow for sin which joyfully accepts salvation by grace.
      Sorrow for sin leading to future obedience.
   2. The sorrow of the world is—
      Caused by shame at being found out;
      Is attended by hard thoughts of God;
      Leads to vexation and sullenness;
      Incites to hardening of heart;
      Lands the soul in despair;
      Works death of the worst kind.
      This needs to be repented of, for it is in itself sinful and leads inexorably to more sin.

III. **Indulge Ourselves in Godly Sorrow for Sin.**
   Come, let us be filled with a wholesome grief that we:

1. Have broken a law, pure and perfect.
2. Have disobeyed a gospel, divine and gracious.
3. Have grieved a God, good and glorious.
4. Have slighted Jesus, whose love is tender and boundless.
5. Have been ungrateful, though loved, elected, redeemed, forgiven, justified and soon to be glorified.

A cognate text in Romans. 2:2, 4, will help us here. These two allied but distinct intimations may be placed in parallel lines, and treated like an equation; thus—

"The goodness of God leadeth thee to repentance."

"Godly sorrow worketh repentance."

- We learn, as the result of the comparison, that the goodness of God leads to repentance by the way of godly sorrow. The series of cause and effect runs thus: goodness of God; godly sorrow; repentance.

  Do not mistake; a fear of hell is not sorrow for sin; it may be nothing more than a regret that God is holy.

  So hard is a heart long accustomed to evil, that nothing can melt it but goodness; and no goodness but God's; and no goodness of His but the greatest. Thanks be to God for His unspeakable gift. "Looking unto Jesus" is the grand specific for producing godly sorrow in a human heart.

  It was a hard heart that quivered under the beams of His loving eye on the threshold of Pilate's judgment hall. When Jesus looked on Peter, Peter went out and wept. Emmanuel's love has lost none of its melting power; the hardest hearts laid fairly open to it must ere long flow down. God's goodness, embodied in Christ crucified, becomes, under the ministry of the Spirit, the cause of the godly sorrow in believing men.— William Arnot.

- Sin, repentance, and pardon are like to the three vernal months of the year, March, April and May. Sin comes in like March, blustering, stormy, and full of bold violence. Repentance succeeds like April, showering, weeping, and full of tears. Pardon follows like May, springing, singing, full of joy and flowers. Our eyes must be full of *April*, with the sorrow of repentance; and then our hearts shall be full of *May*, with the true joy of forgiveness. —Thomas Adams
C.H. SPURGEON

SOWING AND REAPING

"Be not deceived; God is not mocked: for whatsoever a man soweth, that shall he also reap" (Galatians 6:7).

I. God Is Not to Be Trifled With.
1. Either by the notions that there will be no rewards and punishments.
2. Or by the idea that a bare profession will suffice to save us.
3. Or by the fancy that we shall escape in the crowd.
4. Or by the superstitious supposition that certain rites will set all straight at last, whatever our lives may be.

II. The Laws of His Government Cannot Be Set Aside.
1. It is so in nature. Law is inexorable. Gravitation crushes the man who opposes it.
2. It is so in providence. Evil results surely follow social wrong.
3. Conscience tells us it must be so. Sin must be punished.

III. Evil Sowing Will Bring Evil Reaping.
1. This is seen in the present result of certain sins.
   Sins of lust bring disease into our bodies.
   Sins of idolatry have led men to cruel and degrading practices.
   Sins of temper have caused murders, wars, strifes and misery.
   Sins of appetite, especially drunkenness, cause want, misery, delirium, etc.
2. This is seen when the sinner becomes himself disappointed in the result of his conduct.
   His malice eats his heart; his greed devours his soul; his infidelity destroys his comfort; his raging passions agitate his spirit.

IV. Good Sowing Will Bring Good Reaping.
1. What are its seeds?
   Toward *God*—we sow in the Spirit, faith and obedience.
   Toward *men*—love, truth, justice, kindness, forbearance.
   Toward *self*—control of appetite, purity, etc.
2. What is the reaping of the Spirit?
Life everlasting dwelling within us and abiding there forever.

It is not an open question at all whether I shall sow or not today; the only question to be decided is: Shall I sow good seed or bad? Every man always is sowing for his own harvest in eternity either tares or wheat. According as a man soweth, so shall he also reap; he that sows the wind of vanity shall reap the whirlwind of wrath.

- Suppose a man should collect a quantity of small gravel and dye it carefully, so that it should resemble wheat, and sow it in his fields in spring, expecting that he would reap a crop of wheat like his neighbor's in the harvest. The man is mad; he is a fool to think that by this silly trick he can evade the laws of nature, and mock nature's God.

  Yet equally foolish is the conduct, and far heavier the punishment, of the man who sows wickedness now, and expects to reap safety at last. Sin is not only profitless and disastrous; it is eminently a deceitful work. Men do not of set purpose cast themselves away; sin cheats a sinner out of his soul.

  But sowing righteousness is never, and nowhere, lost labor. Every act done by God's grace, and at His bidding, is living and fruitful. It may appear to go out of sight, like seed beneath the furrow; but it will rise again. Sow on Christians! Sight will not follow the seed far; but when sight fails, sow in faith, and you will reap in joy soon. —William Arnot

- Doth any think he shall lose by his charity? No worldling, when he sows his seed, thinks he shall lose his seed; he hopes for increase at harvest. Darest thou trust the ground, and not God? Sure God is a better paymaster than the earth; grace doth give a larger recompense than nature. Below, thou mayest receive forty grains for one; but in heaven (by the promise of Christ) a hundred-fold: a measure heaped, and shaken, and thrust together, and yet running over.

  "Blessed is he that considereth the poor"; there is the seeding: "The Lord shall deliver him in the time of trouble" (Ps. 41:1); there is the harvest. Is that all? No! Matthew 25:35: "Ye fed Me when I was hungry, and gave Me drink when thirsty"— comforted Me in misery; there is the sowing. *Venite, beati.* "Come, ye blessed of My Father, inherit the kingdom prepared for you"; there is the harvest. —Thomas Adams
  C.H. SPURGEON

SINNERS BROUGHT NIGH

"But now in Christ Jesus, ye who sometimes were afar off, are made nigh by the blood of Christ" (Ephesians 2:13).

The Ephesian Christians, previous to their conversion, were Gentiles, v. 11; and thus were aliens from the commonwealth of Israel, and strangers from the covenants of promise, v. 12. The prophets had foretold that Jesus should be given "for a light to the Gentiles"—for God's salvation to the ends of the earth, Isaiah 49:6. Jesus came—the Gentiles were enlightened; the ends of the earth saw the salvation of God; and "in Christ Jesus those who had been far off, were made nigh by the blood of Christ."

I. We Were Sometimes Far Off.

This intimates *distance*, and signifies that we were ignorant of God, chap. 4:18. Destitute of His image, chap. 5:22-24. Under His displeasure, chap. 2:1-3. Unconnected with His church. v. 11,12.

What a significant idea! How far were we from a true, an experimental knowledge, of God—of the things of God: how far from any resemblance to His moral image. And we were equally distant from His church—His people.

The apostle's words include another idea connected with this distance; namely, the time.

Ye were *sometimes* far off. It was with many of us a long time; with all a *miserable* time, and a *dangerous* time. But thanks be to God! these times are passed away; our text says ye *were* far off.

Here let us pause, and think on what we *were*. Some of us were lost in the cares of the world. Some were deluded by the deceitfulness of riches. The lust of other things held some captive. While others were intoxicated by pleasure, or enchanted by worldly science, or drawn away by the meaner things which attract the attention of sordid souls. It is enough, more than enough, *that we were far from God*. Let us now turn our attention to our present situations.

II. Now Are We Made Nigh.

These words convey to the mind, ideas of *Relationship—Friendship—Union—*and *Communion*.

Relationship. Real Christians are children of God, 2 Cor. 6:17,18; Gal. 3:26. They are brethren, Matthew 23:8. And they are as properly related, in a religious or spiritual sense, both to God and to each other, as men are related to each other by natural ties, see John 1:12,13; Gal. 3:26.

Friendship. Among men of the world, all relatives are not friends; but Christians are in a state of friendship with God, with Christ, and with each other, John 15:14,15; 1 John 3:14.

Union. Jesus is the vine; Christians are the branches, John 15:5. He is the body; they are the members, chap. 5:30. They are the members, too, one of another, Romans 12:5; 1 Corinthians 12:12,13. Again, they are represented as stones of the same building, Jesus being the chief corner stone, vv. 19-22.

Communion. They have relationship with God, as a child with his parent, Romans 8:15; Galatians 4:6, as a man with his friend. They have communion with each other, see 1 John 1:3, 6, 7; Colossians 3:16.

Thus we are made nigh; and our text leads us in the next place to consider how this blessed, this important change has been effected.

III. In Christ Jesus—by the Blood of Christ.

In Christ Jesus. He is our Mediator; God with God; man with men, see 1 Timothy 2:5; Hebrews 12:24.

It is here the distant parties meet. Here the Gentile meets the Jew, v. 14. Here the returning sinner meets a gracious, a merciful, a forgiving God, chap. 1:6,7 and v. 18.

By the blood of Christ. Under the old dispensation, this blood was yearly typified by that of the paschal lamb, Exodus 12:4,5; 1 Corinthians 5:7;—daily by that of the sacrificial lamb, Exodus 29:38,39; John 1:29;—and frequently by that of other sacrifices, Hebrews 9 and 10. Covenants were ratified by blood, Exodus 24:8; Hebrews 9:18-20; "and without shedding of blood is no remission," Hebrews 9:22. "We enter into the holiest by the blood of Jesus," Hebrews 10:19. Almost every important circumstance connected with our salvation has reference to the blood of Christ. We are *redeemed* by His blood, chap. 1:7; Colossians 1:14; 1 Peter 1:19; Revelation 5:9. *Justified* by His blood, Romans 5:9; *washed, cleansed* by His blood, 1 John 1:7; Revelation 1:5, and 7:14; *we conquer* through His blood, Revelation 12:11; *we are made nigh by His blood.*

The shedding of the blood of Christ was the last grand act, as a sacrifice for the sins of mankind; a sacrifice, without which we could have no hope; without which we must have perished, Acts 4:10, 12. Well then, may such frequent mention be made of the *blood of Christ*. There is no reconciliation with God but by the *blood of Jesus.*   CHARLES SIMEON